Rising About Us

Rising About Us

EDITH VAN BEEK

Netherlandic Press, 1994
Windsor, Ontario

CANADIAN CATALOGUING
IN PUBLICATION DATA

Van Beek, Edith
  Rising about us

Poems.
ISBN 0-919417-34-5

I. Title.

PS8593.A5383R5 1994   C811'.54
C94-931833-7
PR9199.3.V35R5 1994

Published by Netherlandic Press, P.O. Box
396, Station A, Windsor, Ontario, Canada
N9A 6L7.

The publisher wishes to acknowledge the
generous financial support of the Canada
Council and the Ontario Arts Council –
Joan Magee, Publisher.

Thanks to Gerard Brender à Brandis for his
permission to reproduce the wood engraving
'Tulip' on the back cover of this book.

The cover is from the painting,
Rising About Us, by John Van Beek.
Photo credit: Rick Masters.

to John

CONTENTS

Morning's Blood

BIRTHING

My mother rocked on the porch
that seaside morning
after my brother was cut
from her belly like a rose.

He died from a swollen head,
water-on-the-brain.
I imagined him floating
over the sea, a pink balloon
on the cord of her pain,
his body beating like a boat
against the tide.

Water fell from her face
where apple blossoms drifted
over our garden like spits
of the sea.

CANNING

Mother sweat with tomatoes
alive in our sink, scarlet,
ready for skinning.
I promised myself; no veggie
would ever drag me down
in the heat.

Glasses filled with flesh
of the fruit were bottled
for winter. My father
carried baskets of rubies
into the kitchen
and she held them
underwater like organ transplants,
her apron scarred with tissue
and seeds that summer
when veggies took over;
made us their slaves.

I swore I'd never marry a man
who gardened for more than a salad,
for more than a meal.

RETURNING

Fifty years later, we foot
a path to the beach
moving into the marsh
between cottages growing
out of old dunes
into backyards, hoping
our heads will not betray us.

Stretched to a towel's length
we're easy with the world
where tides suck in and gulls
sail sheets of sea.

We find lucky stones, lifelines
running through their heads,
a dead seabird lost in its wings,
a graveyard where dead wait
for stones; ghosts of the past,
a woman with a small girl
searching for her son;
my mother, me.

Now, rocks fence one beach
from another; barriers
we no longer believe in.

Grubs, aphids, weevils and rollers,
mites, earwigs, hoppers and slugs
eating thumbs off runners
of strawberry plants; berries
believing in sun.
Stones among leaves, this idea
of berries, our need for colour,
our need for summer,
bits of red on the lips.

My father grew berries
larger than noses, redder
than blood running from spring
into summer, from table to mouth;
my father the bug killer,
the chemical man, god of sevin,
rotenone and malathion, murdering
strawberry lovers to bring thumbs
to our tongues.

MENTOR

My father moves through corn
in old overalls, soft thuds
of a hoe like apples falling
or the talk of a clock, hands
caught in calculated breaths.
He laughs his wild interruptive
laugh, corn stuck between teeth.
In the photo, his white hair
fills the sky. Everything
moves towards harvest.

In my dream we are driving
down a railroad track, words
printed on him, a newspaper
we stuff under the seat.
We hear a train; he quotes
another poem.

He's in love with the way
my mother believes in him;
simplicity, a pattern he cuts
from cloth. In love with time,
he's afraid of losing it.
At the end, another day
is too much to live up to.

This photo can't hold the sun;
it escapes, a grosbeak on a branch
who draws us in and is gone.
Each day new suns appear,
there's no end to fires
beyond us.

My father died by his own hands,
we couldn't stop them
from drowning the light.
I ran through the house
and broke all his clocks.
Through a tear in his pants
I saw his skin,
the patch on his face
the undertaker missed,
rose like a scar.

I write by the garden,
my flesh is falling, I grow old.
Here a tree I love is downed
and piled for fire; my father's
body. Already it sends
from the stump, new shoots –
nature trying to make itself
again.

AFTER THE SURGERY

After the surgery,
a neighbour said you wept
alone in the house;
she brought you lunch
as you lay with the sheet
a quiet water below your neck,
your eyes, wet stones.

I was a child, what did
I know of holding on?
That one day you'd let go
behind my back and leave
me here in the sea
of your making.

In the Cape house
of childhood, I dream
cylindrical rooms,
down narrow stairs
to the rising tide.
Daddy is here in white
where I wait in the eye
of the wind. He leaves
as he lived, without words.
Where the sea takes all
in its path, I walk alone
with the facts.

Daddy drives over roads
of chain. I hike a beach
of bears who lie
on their backs, paws
in the air, a bedful
of teddies.
By daddy's laughter I see
it's a joke – his driving
the hard way forward,
the cruel way back.

Mother opens a map;
she's lost, her mouth
can't be stilled.
We drive on nothing but dreams;
daddy bursts into poems, he weeps
and clicks his tongue.

We're the past of ourselves
moving up and down the same
histories looking for doors.
Daddy watches, his blue eyes
wet and hurt. He knows
I will disown him by my words.

He reads his eulogy
among our trees, he removes
his clothes wanting to fly
or fall he cannot do both.

Here in a hospice of waking
a storm darkens the day.
Daddy looks for his home,
stairs people enter and exit,
never meeting again. Books
he gathers aren't his,
children he touches grow
old. He pushes a car
he no longer drives
downstairs we no longer climb
towards a rising tide.

EULOGY

His wit sizzled,
icicles thrown
on a skillet.
They hang now,
his similies
cool as glass
where nothing
moves this space
but the sorrow
of his laughing face
passing in an ocean
wind as bubbles
of the blower's breath.

He fell birch
painted white
upon the wood,
a book mark
passes on
but not a book.
When space can seize
his thoughts
I write the living
of his tree.

THE RULES

Stand up and be counted
my father told us
as if we were Dutch Elms.

Don't tell lies, my mother
said, don't call WOLF
like the boy in the tale
minding his sheep.

Watch your words, said uncle,
or the dragonfly will lock
your lips with his needle;
suture your voice.

Don't play with fire,
aunties warned us, keep
your eyes on your wings
like a moth in the light.
Beware of boys with matches
looking for smoke; wayward
girls with burn in their skirts.

CLOISTERED

She watches the swing
move on its chain,
the seesaw filling the sky
with its reliable slant.
When the monkey bars
turn her upside down
she wants the world
as safe as a sandbox
filled with the toys
of her necessary life.

This man's a clock;
he wants his life
like a cupboard;
plates piled, cups
hung. He watches her
boil berries, ripe
as hearts and crush
them alive. He doesn't know
her talent for metaphor.

CUPS

White hollyhocks
stand in our garden,
cups in a stack
like the ones you made
for our wedding –
broken over the years.

We have one cup left,
my husband's for coffee;
he drinks from your hands.
We live as hollyhocks
on a windless morning,
stacked for breaking.

Latitudes

GOODBYES

My mother's eyes ran over
her mail order coat;
dad mumbled wise words;
nail punctures.

On the train
I slumped by the window
and watched them fade
on an edge of evening
standing near the tracks
waiting for the whistle
to do them in.

It was myself
I said goodbye to,
unaware just then;
relieved and scared to see
how easily I made two people
vanish by stretching out
the landscape.

I wonder what it was
that needed leaving,
testing their insignificance
against my own.
Taking myself on that journey,
I took them too.

CONFINED

Through that aquarium
sun grew an eye,
bubbles caught my breath.
I swam, a salmon to light,
longing to be a gull, to plunge
where blue skin hid
sea creatures in the spinning
earth, two cups joined
at the lips, a beachball
caught in a net of longitudes
and latitudes –
as if lines could set me free.

STATISTICS

Over the ocean
two planes collide,
people swim
in their red balloons.
Nothing can stop
the breaking,
the swallowing,
the planes corkscrew
to the sea, this whale
of water where they go
to bubbles.
Waves do their best
to keep things clean
as the numbers round
themselves off.

REBIRTH

Leave this spaceship
over earth in its shroud
where land forms spread;
America, Africa, Eurasia
growing a field for harvest,
the southern icecap
floating like a swan.

Reach out, sink like a speck
in the sea's womb, like dust
into roots of trees.
Enter again an invisible cell.

Inhabit this blue stone,
move on its eye, its spill
of poles; this is the way
light gathers its long chapters.

Over the planet's flesh
rides a sky so thin
that stars fire through
on their journeys, one
metamorphosis after another.

DYLAN THOMAS

In Swansea
tumbling out of the park,
your ball reaches earth,
bouncing over and over
this tent-shaped, rick-rack,
roof-tip town.

At Fernhill
leaves bear summer away,
stone owls perch in shadows
of hours. This farm lies
in its robe, folds into fields;
an old gate opens and waits
on its chain.

In Laugharne
your boathouse embraces sea,
walling old wounds;
an estuary tides over flats
to a writing shed, now closed
as your mouth. A cliff hangs
over sky through the holly
and holy of waters.
I'm rooted as the tree
on this hill where your cross
is a seagull home from sailing.

Drinking with cormorants
winging the wharf
among green books of trees,
I feel a wound of words
on the world.

MT. KILIMANJARO

We climb equator to arctic
on this volcanic rise of the rift
open to rainforest and icefield
where we wander the latitudes
rising about us; stark beauty,
sudden as insight, silently gone.

We hike foothills where slaves
once crossed on the blood
of their dying; explorers
trampled red carnelians
under their boots. Through forests
roping with green we trail roots,
bones of earth hanging deep,
primeval.

Flames of flowers turn pale
as we move on this ladder
from heather to moorland.
In red-peppered stone and desert
scree we rest in the shade
of boulders from radiating arms
of sun. You go on when you can't.

One could end here on a rockface,
dangling from a rope, hanging
over terrifying beauty a few hours
before darkness and death.

At the peak we wander
a crater's womb while Africa
spreads her body before us.

THE AFRICA OF ME

The africa of me
is in a cat's night;
leaves are singing
in the moving dark,
everything has eyes.

I bring you down
to clothe my body
with your love
under the jacaranda;
your sandpaper tongue
grows velvet on my skin,
your paws leave patches
upon my thighs.

Your claws touch
the throat of my cat,
pulse vibrating under
thick fur; your claws
want to go jungle,
want to go wild.

I wear my stripes,
a carnivorous smile.
I know where flesh hides,
I know your taste
is all in your teeth.

SKIDEGATE

Tide comes in greedy
filling hollows with a tongue
bringing life to logs
thrown here for floating
with raven wings; waves
cleaning and cleaning.

A dying grows at sea edge
where slate closes its mouth
shifting stones like baskets
of fish, dunes circle with wood,
stormed trees move like us,
hands between wind.

Here the endless body of water
works around cedar and spruce
taking us in and in to herself,
healing and healing, letting us
out and out as sand.
We are nothing on this bone
of the beach.

POLAR WOMAN

At first sun
after months of moon
she sweeps her igloo
with wings of a gull
where her shoulders
are warmed with caribou
and her baby lies
in his deerskin cap.

Wind's at the back
of her man
preparing the sledge,
snow moves over the ice
like dogs.
The season of darkness
passes at this point
of light.

A mouth of frozen sea
holds us in lips of snow,
gales tunnel us under,
leave our huskies iced.
Deerskin wraps our bodies
where winter trails
our skin, rocks relieve
our eyes. We live
on biscuits, tea, pemmican;
our dogs if it comes to that.

Migrating ice thins
cracking its bone,
a stab of dark cloud
brings us a lead of open
water that could take us in.

We sit out blizzards
in the tent, snow sugars
its way in. In this lunar
light, too cold to sleep
we push on
numbed by polar wind.

Crossing Cape Columbia
we leave the Roosevelt
in floes no comfort
of her belly, no sails
to steer us.

In March leads close
with young ice; we are walk,
tea and shattered sleep
on this glass table top.
Many sleds are broken,
many dogs have died.

April, we arrive at 90°
where all directions
'blend into one.'
After a hoist of our flag
we leave, unable to grasp
this white and holy place.

Island behind island
breaks the arctic sea
where a raven circles
a cliff; a black fan of wings,
white fan of light; beyond
this glacial skin tundra rides
to a fiord jigsawed with ice.
Over moss and stone
ravens head down,
at the point of falling
they grow wings.

No place on earth is unexplored,
untouched by human shoe;
here, a foot has crushed
the saxifrage, left plastic
bags along the shore.

We cannot escape the polar's
claw, the raven's scream
before the unforgiving quiet.

Rising About Us

THE CREDIT

Pulsating over stones,
genesis of fields,
this nomadic hand
pleasures birds
opening wings of water.

Holding a heron at dawn
this river transforms
into journey,
if only in our eyes.

We are safe here,
we know where we are
winging under the sun,
longing to ride
over bodies of stones,
old selves we shed
for flight.

Ice cracks the river
where water runs,
black silk below glass.

Blood orbits a body,
a heart like a star;
a brain floats
in its dark bowl
where time clocks on
and light follows
the sky.

Morning melts into noon.
Season slides into season,
sun counts its hours,
raising and lowering
its beautiful blood.

SONGBIRDS

Songbirds searching for blueberries,
boxberries, bearberries, bunchberries,
barberries, bayberries, blackberries,
bilberries and bloodberries call
in the bush for lovers
and fledglings, the joy of sun
on wings from treetops, bushtops
and canetips edging the sky.

We are searching the woods
for the tastiest, brightest
and biggest; we've been raised
on labels, skin and flesh
of the fruit, a sweetness of breath
for berries in bunches, in boxes
wanting blood for our songs.

Where the bird bath
blooms a giant mushroom
the field opens its green
to the long sky, squirrels
carry apples in their mouths.

We know the trees to go
naked, those that will hold
in the eye of the wind.

Cardinals will arrive
at dusk in their reds,
night pulling its sweater
over trees.
We know the snow that rests
in the garden will bring
flowers to match their names.

SHORT DAYS

My mother mourns briefly,
flies into a new day
where December turns
each morning into song.

Off on whistling wings
a mourning dove ooo's
beyond marigold beds
under winter's white.

A pine siskin voices
to a hip of river
where snow mounds;
wind muting every scratch
of track
in momentary passing.

IT'S HER TIME, she says
as each friend drops
from sight; as if each
mourning is a dove
returning over beds
of summer.

TRANSIENCE

Colour turns the sky;
a monarch born in the garden
dries its wings.

My hair grows from a branch
where I've clung all summer.
Above, each star, an eye
of someone gone, faces
in old photos speak and leave
before we hear them.

No bird knows the tree
where each gathers
for the journey
in this country of fire.

Wind casts in the birds
picks up their small truths,
ice speaks continually
of spring; many sleeps at end.
Trees get ideas of being green,
she-birds cradle in the sun,
swinging – something I loved
as a child, back and forth
my mind free while my body
busied with a known thing.

On windy nights birches rub
against the house
asking to come in, swinging
at the window like hung men.

Evenings I walk by the river
to get away from myself,
to swing into the body
of something larger, breathing
what everything breathes
in the wind's eye. My mind
flags this river like a boat,
unsure where the water ends.

All night in the eye of the wind
stars walk their dark road,
a moon shadow wheels with wings
of a giant moth.

At dawn, when birds begin, I feel
as fragile as everything that stops.

NOVEMBER NIGHT

November night;
wind ties pine
to larch where we lie
in the dark
hearing click-clacks
of branches pressing
on each other's wood.

I wonder where whitetails
sleep, when the buck
arrives at dawn,
hoof scratching a shag
of leaves, rubbing
antlers over bark,
leaving his scars.

I wake in your arms,
you stroke my back,
I feel a sharp press
of autumn underskin,
the heart laid bare.

Red continents
spread over this planet
of green skin.
Hanging from its pole
the texture of landscape
is monotonous.
There are no seasons
but summer
for the brevity
of its dance.

SLICING

A swallow knifes the wind,
an apple tree spills petals
hunched in our garden
working for fruit.

Hard rounds button the tree,
songs of small things.
Inside, seeds press against
their summer flesh
hanging from arms bracelets
of fruit, our tree killing
light, apples ending
their rounds.

We journey into apples,
throw away their stars
before wind talks them off
branches, swallows
out of summer.

Remember when you cut
this apple, I'm inside.

CIRCLES OF SILENCE

We are learning how to live
among trees, only they can save us
from the sky with their vision
of light; branches new with summer
growing leaves in our flesh.

Trees hear all we have to say,
years of wind in their bark
where a moon wanders,
its large mouth thinning
by morning to faint hairs.

Where we go is hidden from us;
none knows earth who created us
where each dreams of solitude,
lights in circles of silence.

We hope for more than there is,
we cannot grieve deeply as trees
nor take as long to pass away.

MOONSONG

You dress in white
round belly
at my window
waiting to be stroked;
there's so much
between us.
Even a song
won't carry my voice.
You have me waiting
at my window
while you wink
at night and poke
bright fingers
through my hair,
one endless rope
of light.

This pale balloon among stars
building a shadow
makes a flag of the earth.

Our eyes sense distance,
shifts of light between stars
and moon. Faces hide
what we see reflecting
a lifetime, shadows crossing
scarves of night, one body
blocking another.

This is the eclipse we walk
a country road to see,
so few in a century naked
by light where stone moves
into stone.

Circling, you hold this field
in your eyes; ragged wings,
king of the sky. Visioning
the smallest flight,
the most insignificant star,
nothing escapes your telescope,
your beak hooking over
long claws catching us up
in time, soaring beyond
the first bird's kreee –
raptor of small choices;
clutching us now at the close
of this millennium
with our boots off
in the black holes
of our miscalculations.

Circling this universe
from a treetip of the mind,
hawk king of the sky
rides invisible stars,
words he forms in his head,
whistles, squeaks
in the language of deaf,
starblind, earthbound fledglings
with launch on our brains.

'NOBODY SEES A FLOWER'
– G. O'Keeffe

Georgia, what is it about this poppy
that cannot last, firey wings
on the heat of a ragged afternoon
turned dead soldier, black for a heart?

What is it you say through the purple
poise of the petunia in her five
fluted skirt, trumpeting
the soft side of her landscape
down in those dark rooms?

Would we miss the sweet pea's vulva
or the sun on the tongue of an iris
if you hadn't forced us into the eyes
of a moth?

RED ROSES

Red roses, thrown in the ravine,
celebrate the child who died
last winter; her heart crushed
by a train, girl blood on snow.

This man who accidently hurled
his daughter to her death,
returns, his arms full of red
redemption where unrelenting
lines of track slash snow
and stones fall off on either side,
tossing themselves in the river
running open, a dark wound.

Wanting The Light

VAN GOGH

Wind runs
through the garden
slanting all
to its whim.
Sunflowers
are hanging for rain.
This is the beginning
of the storm
he has painted;
this is the map
of his going.

If yellow is the colour
of madness
then bring on the flowers,
the rough cut flip-flop
yarn of the brush
yearning to the last seed
in a trial by flower
modeled on sun in swollen
joy.
If yellow is the colour
of madness
Van Gogh begs for light.
Tearing the sky down
he yells his years
in the burning blaze
of a yellowed star.

THE LIGHT

Turner cried out
THE LIGHT, THE LIGHT —
longing to catch sun
in his hands, his eyes
to make it last.

The best line God wrote,
LET THERE BE LIGHT —
out of those words
rocks appeared; cells
waited for water,
waited for warmth.

Turner died mixing
the perfect white,
brushing his canvas
with the colour of stars.

WATERLILIES

(C. Monet)

Morning opens the pond
transforming night cloth
into emerald flames,
cascading willows
in a glaze of light;
branches stitched in water
are ripped and stitched again.
Each leaf tips into luminous
fire; waterdrops, watercolours,
waterlilies cupping themselves
into white. Sun shimmers
pass prism's edge between change.
Now, is all there is.

STONE HOUSES

(To speak of the dead is to make them
live again: *Charles Wright*)

My uncle
drives through the graveyard
where my grandparents live
in bones of marriage.

He points out his plot
by river willows
as if he will know,
when he's dead,
how water sings under stones.

We talk of the dead,
my uncle and I; they rise
as willows before us
where the river speaks.

No one knows the stone houses
we live in.

KEW GARDENS

Leaving you wrapped in a navy coat
I move over perfect grass –
you become a blue dot where light
falls over great arms of exotic
evergreens embracing earth and sky
as if the landscape would dissolve
without them.

In your eyes, I too become a dot
on the edge of spring
where lilac fragrance lingers
among rhododendrons in expectant
pinks. What is it we expect
of each other, now that we age
in this splendour soaking up light
among careful trees, gardens
pregnating spaces before us?

What more do you expect than nurture
in your last years or I of you
than a heart to hear my silence?
Each tree still has its time,
each lilac its May, each one
who moves away has already left
a dot.

YOU'RE THE MOTHER NOW, you say
as roses unfold before us
and I lead you back to the city
as if you are the child –
past blue iris yawning in the park
under dove-happy trees;
this ending, another day away.

(1350 BC) What sticks out
is cut off; a nose, fingers,
a penis perhaps.
Take this limestone wife
for instance – her hands
and breasts knocked off
while her man stares into light,
aloof in his stone. And she,
like the good wife, suffers
in silence, knowing the cost
of each breast, the missing
work of her hands
among hieroglyphic birds
who walk the walls.

CECROPIA

A cocoon,
attached to our gate,
dies in its armour,
a moth in a wave of wings.

My aunt, in her bed
by the sea, waits
for her body, an eggshell
under a sheet.

    Here, with her sisters
    in this old photo
    each wears a butterfly bow.
    Here, she holds me,
    and here, she encircles
    her parents, dressed
    in her traveling suit.

Hidden under this sheet
death weaves its cocoon
where she will pull herself free
and wing into light.

MY DEATH

I want to enjoy my death,
pack for the trip, tracks
leading to sunlight
so brilliant I see all colours,
all the good I've ever done
as I drown in last hours
of air, returning; a bird
perching in my ears
like music, the softest part
of me rising, searching
a way back to clouds.

THE WINDOW

Near the window which holds me
away from the world, I learn
how to listen. What does it mean,
this death; the leap from the sill
we all take?

At the bus station we clutch
a ticket and wait under a clock
for the right gate. Ride out
to a good death; let trees rush by,
see beyond glass where the sky
doesn't end.

FOR CHARLIE

It's autumn, we remember
your words – 'the trees
are crying.'

Your mother has turned
inward her tears, her pen
flows over paper.

Your father is silent
as a lake where life
falls early, floating
on water; your breath.

Your brother drifts by
in his car, he knows
in his head you are dead
but his love still looks
for you.

SAN LUIS REY

(for Merci)

San Luis Rey spreads shoulders
over this country; monks
slip by in their robes
where trees drop petals
in the night.

Under the pepper tree
you step in sandals,
your life, flagstones
under your feet.
Lost in the death of your child
you hold this cloistering star
that gives light to roses
at the end of the path
where an iron gate penetrates
your heart.

You speak to me
like your cat, concisely;
you're used to your lap.
You say we are old,
years sit on your mind.
There's no turning back
in our country;
the path erases behind us
like a trail in the wind.
Your death talk
is deep talk
and I don't want to fall in.

(for Diana)

In this lake of my life
your coming brings out
the loon in me, my tongue
dragging word loss,
this red-eyed shrill
I hold inside, your poems
echoing as you pass
this mirror before us,
your head smooth as stone.

I like to think of us
driving north,
you cutting silence
with unstoppable songs.
I swim the distance
between us; you rejoice
in the dark.

In this lake of my life
star pictures dance –
Orion, Taurus, the dippers
working their way above
your gallery where dead stars
paint water and wood
close to the moon's white hand.

In the morgue they tag bodies
with labels like packets
of seed, catalogued; each
for its place in the earth.

Seeing the embalmer's bottle,
blood spirals the body,
a jugular sucks up water,
machinery of death.
Flesh could be closed
in a box like Sleeping Beauty
feeding roots of trees.

A mahogany urn seals us in
after the fire when we shrink
into stones and live on a bookcase
like words.

A SHEET

A sheet
is all it takes
to divide
lovers.

Dark moves
our minds
to separate
rooms.

The sheet
which covers
one of us
is serious.

BLACK HOLES

They pull you in
with their arms,
death dressed up as night
over the city
you live in, each street
a stranger, each streetlight
buzzing like a brain
in its basket of dark.

This hole your mother
digs in her heart
when your father dies;
she opens herself to space
you dare not fly into,
quicksand, quicksilver,
a mirror swallows you –
a pond at the edge
of December still waits
for ice.

Darkness widens,
takes you in, a cave
in the drop of evening
all the city lights
cannot suppress.

Light opens trees
to the air's breath;
ascending, descending,
bringing all into waking
at line's edge, each stroke
of grass, a piece of sky.

Light is the last we know
before we sleep, we die
and wake breathing sky,
the love of line
where we reach out,
pressing all it closes in,
taking us over the distance
we want to go.

ESCALATIONS

Two college boys
play war games in the woods.
One squats with a gun clicking,
the other wears bush brown;
red paint is scribbled
on his back – blood,
the price of war
depending on the moves
of these boys at the edge
of the track where trains
cross Canada a few times
a week; here the horizon
keeps clicking back,
sky reddens with blood;
here small wars begin.

Ethiopians have nowhere to go,
their skulls perch, oversized
eggs on bundles of sticks.
No Ozymandias here! Nothing
to break a dying land
with a mark of importance.

Strapped to their seats
500 Japanese students climb;
no one knows they will plunge
like swallows, meet a mountain
and melt like Hiroshima.

Sun falls yawning fire;
tree scars bloom in a desert
of sky. Here in Polynesia –
newborn jellyfish babies
lie in transparent skins.

'It's safe here to test
the bomb.'

Tents are lines on a desert
strewn with skulls,
maracas of wind.
Camels kneel in corpses
like broken dhows. Sun blinks,
a cat's eye, a yellow bubble,
a swallowed dot. No one is left
to see the light go to pieces
in their soft eyes.

Two college boys
play war games in the woods ...

ANNE SEXTON (1928-1974)

I Anne touches
the skin of her doll
born fully clothed,
curls coiffured,
a face as bland
as an apple's.

She enjoys undressing,
what will she see?
A dimple, perhaps,
not the birthcave surely,
but the smooth innocent
flesh in a dress,
the body her mother
desires.

II Anne discovers the exit,
escape from pain, a hegira
back to her mother,
her grandmother
and the mother before that.

My mother and I
return to Cape Cod,
to the old house
in the scrub oak
close to the sea –
wandering like gulls,
our eyes marbled
by memory

where the butterfly
swirls on salt-wind
to the mouth of the rose.

This purse Anne throws
in the Charles River
contains her lipstick,
her rings, blood beads.
Past Mercy Street,
past the brick boxes
of Harvard she dances
in scarlet, all the way
under a water of night.

My mother says, 'blood
is thicker than water' –
it will keep us up.

III Anne rows her boat
on a desert;
sky turns over
trying to rain
on this casket
holding the rose
she's longing to drown.

Rowing towards sky
she believes earth
is round.
She doesn't know
it's a room with a wall,
that she rows on her dying
heart. She doesn't know
these islands are men

she never married
and the sun
is her wedding bed.

IV   The well you searched
and said you found –
what well, Anne?
A word well
surfacing your mind
in its madness,
your poems on the lips
of students who followed
you, like Joan, to the stake?

In this desert an oasis
is marked by a tree –
stop and drink
if you would save your life.

V   Approaching floor 6000
did you expect stars;
hearts waiting to receive
yours? Keys that opened
answers? Envision
an entrance to space
with your name on the door?

Was it glass, that elevator
into the sky? Did you see
everything falling away

into place? Your box
pulled like a casket
out of the earth like S.B.
the fairy tale princess
under her dome?

VI 1970
Sun works Anne over
like a yellow mother,
embracing sand
slipping away like the sea
slips under the moon
messaging a landscape
held in a glass.

It was Nana's leaving
that broke the tree,
drove it down
in the northeaster,
tore off its head
and arms, its insides
egging over the bark
like mucus.

1972
Anne writes in the kitchen,
coffee finds a way in,
words pulse on her stove.
She worked a lifetime
for death, that lean cat
on a branch
where sun falls now
in yellow leaves.

1974
Anne sits in the cougar
in her mother's fur coat
vodka in hand; autumn's embrace
cannot reach her. Night
is a long place.

EDITH VAN BEEK grew up on Cape
Cod. A graduate of Lesley College and
Columbia University, she has taught in
New England, East Africa, the Queen
Charlotte Islands and Ontario where
she lives with her husband, John.
  Her seaside youth, her travels
through England, East Africa and the
Canadian north weave through her
work. Her concise writing style shares
with her readers insights as accessible
as the natural life forms rising about us.

ABOUT THE ARTIST

JOHN VAN BEEK paints portraits for
others. His landscapes, inspired by
dreams, express the sobering realities of
how we mistreat our environment.

In this cover painting, entitled *Rising
About Us*, nature moves above the
clouds in search of unpolluted air.

ACKNOWLEDGEMENTS

Some of these poems have appeared in
the following periodicals: *Amethyst
Review; Arc;* BBC *Wildlife Award;
Canadian Author & Bookman;* CVII;
*Fiddlehead; League of Canadian Poets
Newsletter; Moonstone Press; Newest
Review; Northward Journal;
Orangeville, This Week; Poet's Gallery;
Quarry; Rural Writings; Symposium;
Tower; Womansong; Woman I Am.*